Dear Par

Our 500 Que created for parents and children to have fun together while learning. The book presents material on math, literacy, science, music, social skills, nature, creativity and health – all fundamental to school success. Our questions are lively, enriching and unique, and our bonus riddles add extra learning and laughter!

Building a child's confidence and enthusiasm for learning at an early age is key to future success. It is our sincere hope that the Learnalots™ will inspire children, and those who care for them, to learn something new every day.

– The BrightStart Learning Team

What are germs:
bacteria or bugs?

Which fruit has more potassium:
bananas or oranges?

Which species is the tallest
tree in the world:
sequoia or redwood?

bacteria, bananas, redwood

Does feline refer to dog or cat?

Are anteaters related to sloths or Siberian tigers?

Is a slumber party a sleepover with friends, or a party where people cut trees?

cat, sloths, sleepover with friends

Do strawberries have seeds on the inside or the outside?

How many triangle faces does a pyramid have: four or five?

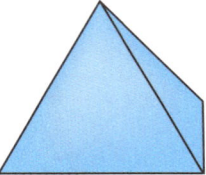

What sport do the Harlem Globetrotters play: baseball or basketball?

outside, four, basketball

Which state is the farthest south in the United States: Minnesota or Texas?

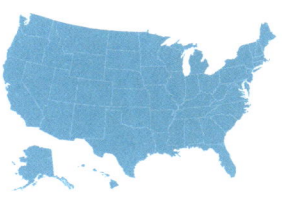

Do bagpipes come from South Africa or Scotland?

Which animals sleeps through the winter: hedgehogs or the hamsters?

Texas, Scotland, hedgehogs

Does accelerate mean to speed up or to slow down?

What is bigger: a crocodile or an alligator?

Is the sun made of hot gas or hot liquid?

speed up, crocodile, hot gas

If you have two dimes and a nickel, how much money do you have: 15 cents or 25 cents?

Do parrots like to imitate or irritate the sounds they hear?

Do olives grow on trees or bushes?

25 cents, imitate, trees

In which sport do you perform the butterfly stroke: tennis or swimming?

In which culture would you wear a lei around your neck: Hawaiian or Chinese?

Are crabs related to spiders or snakes?

swimming, Hawaiian, spiders

Is a cone a 2D shape or a 3D shape?

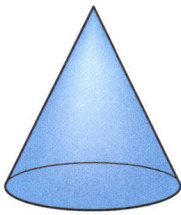

Which word has the letter "U" in it: kitty or puppy?

What do bees take from flowers: nectar or nectarines?

Which instrument is used to measure temperature: a microscope or a thermometer?

Are adults closer to six feet tall or nine feet tall?

Is chocolate made from cocoa beans or cocoa bark?

Why do bees have sticky hair?

Because they use honeycombs!

Are storybooks written by an author or an illustrator?

Do rabbits eat plants or meat?

Which of these is likely magnetic: a boomerang or a pair of scissors?

author, plants, scissors

Which state is the farthest north in the United States: California or Alaska?

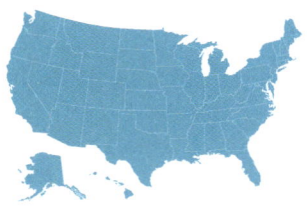

Are kings thought of as regal or common?

What sense do you use when you are eating: sight or taste?

Alaska, regal, taste

Does sugar dissolve
or clump together when
you pour it in water?

Is an herbivore an animal
that eats plants or meats?

If an object is microscopic,
is it really tiny or really hot?

dissolves, plants, really tiny

Which of these words is a noun: sit or chair?

How many sides do most snowflakes have: four or six?

Do snakes shed their tails or their skin?

chair, six, skin

Does the sun rise in the east or the west?

Is the Eiffel Tower located in New York City or Paris, France?

Which word has the letter W in it: towel or shovel?

east, Paris, towel

Which happens at the end of the day: sunset or sunrise?

What shape is Earth: a cone or a sphere?

Would a plumber fix your roof or your toilet?

sunset, sphere, toilet

Which animal can be used for transportation: a leopard or a camel?

Which bird lays the largest egg in the world: an ostrich or a penguin?

Do zoologists study animals or plants?

camel, ostrich, animals

Are briefcases used to hold paper or parakeets?

Which animal can't stick out its tongue: a crocodile or a chameleon?

Which part of your body is important for balance: your ears or your stomach?

paper, crocodile, ears

Is the Mariana Trench a large cave or the deepest place in the ocean?

Are picky eaters referred to as finicky or winicky?

What is in the opposite direction of west: south or east?

Which is the fastest dog in the world: the Greyhound or the Dalmatian?

How many legs do centipedes have: 6 or 100?

Do farmers work in agriculture or architecture?

Greyhound, 100, agriculture

What are the strongest creatures in the ocean?

Mussels!

Which animals hold hands at night so they don't drift apart: otters or octopuses?

In the sport of bowling, does a strike refer to knocking down six pins or ten pins?

Is a bamboo stick really strong or really weak?

otters, ten pins, strong

Does the taste of honey change depending on the flowers used to make it or the time of year it is made?

Do you get confidence from completing a task or quitting a task?

Are spiders arachnids or insects?

Which animal can hide inside
its shell for protection:
a sea turtle or a tortoise?

Which sea animal makes pearls:
an oyster or a sea cucumber?

Do genies
live in
a bottle
or a jar?

tortoise, oyster, bottle

27

Are a bird's bones hollow or solid?

Which is stronger than brick: wood or cement?

Does an umpire work at a sports game or a courtroom?

hollow, cement, sports game

Does gigantic mean
very small or very large?

Does accumulate mean
to collect or to give away?

Does Jack Frost
make snow
or ice cream?

very large, collect, snow

Which animal has webbed wings: a bat or an owl?

Does cotton come from a plant or an animal?

When two musicians play together, is it called a solo or a duet?

bat, plant, duet

Does checkers require
two players or four players?

Does evaporate mean to get
dirty or to turn water into gas?

Do sand dollars come from
sea urchins or sea stars?

two, turn water into gas, sea urchins

31

If you were on a safari, would you ride in a boat or in a jeep?

Do piranha fish have sharp teeth or sharp noses?

Does silk come from worms or from snakes?

jeep, sharp teeth, worms

Does bath water get hotter or colder the longer you sit in it?

Is the pupil a part of your ears or your eyes?

Is a traditional Hawaiian party called a luau or an aloha?

colder, eyes, luau

33

What sport is a combination of soccer and baseball: softball or kickball?

Which is larger: a boat or a ship?

Does absorb mean to soak up liquid or to leak liquid?

kickball, ship, soak up

How do you make seven an even number?

You take the "S" off!

Seven

Are fossils at least
100 years old or at least
10,000 years old?

Are dinosaur bones
ancient or modern?

Which animal has four
stomachs: cows or koalas?

10,000 years old, ancient, cows

What do you call the moon when it is a big, bright circle: a new moon or a full moon?

Is a salamander a lizard or a bird?

Does multiply mean to increase or to decrease?

full moon, lizard, increase

Is California a
state or a country?

Does the constellation Ursa Major
mean big gorilla or big bear?

Do caterpillars have 12 eyes or 2?

state, big bear, 12

Does incline refer to an upward angle or a downward angle?

Which letter is a consonant: I or J?

Do sneezes occur in your sinus or throat?

upward, J, sinus

Which continent is also a country: Canada or Australia?

Which word has more A's: abracadabra or Argentina?

Which animal is said to be able to predict the end of winter: a bear or a groundhog?

Australia, abracadabra, groundhog

Which liquid do humans need to survive: milk or water?

What does "amigo" mean in the Spanish language: friend or taco?

Which animal lives in the water: a possum or an otter?

42

water, friend, otter

Does a biologist study rocks or living things?

Which animal has longer ears: a rabbit or a cat?

Which is the biggest desert in the world: the Sahara or the Arabian?

living things, rabbit, Sahara

43

Is Thanksgiving in the fall or in the spring?

Is tea made from plants or animals?

What color is your blood: blue or red?

fall, plants, red

44

How long does it take for the moon to go around the Earth: one month or one year?

Were sandwiches invented by the Earl of Sandcastle or the Earl of Sandwich?

Which animal is nocturnal: a bat or a crow?

one month, Earl of Sandwich, bat

If you cut a pizza into thirds, do you have two pieces or three pieces?

Do hedgehogs have poor eyesight or poor smell?

Does the Earth rotate around the sun, or does the sun rotate around the Earth?

three, eyesight, Earth rotates around the sun

Why do birds fly south for the winter?

Because it's too far to walk.

Do people get goosebumps when they are hot or when they are cold?

Is spaghetti sauce made from tomatoes or strawberries?

How many teeth do most adults have: 32 or 52?

cold, tomatoes, 32

49

Do ladybugs eat aphids or apples?

Which country is known for having a lot of windmills: The Netherlands or Canada?

Which is closer to earth: the moon or the sun?

aphids, The Netherlands, moon

When someone dresses up, do they look fabulous or delicious?

What is a passport used for: traveling outside the country or checking out books from the library?

Is the bow of the boat the front of the boat or the back of the boat?

fabulous, traveling, front

Would you use a telescope to look at constellations or mold?

Do armadillos have sharp spikes or a hard shell on their backs?

Which is the only food that never spoils: honey or chicken?

constellations, hard shell, honey

Is a frog a reptile or an amphibian?

How many days are in a year: 275 or 365?

Do frilled lizards open their frills to scare predators or catch bugs?

amphibian, 365, scare predators

Do giraffes clean theirs ears with their tongues or their tails?

What is used to keep a boat in place: the brakes or an anchor?

Does hyperactive mean high energy or low energy?

tongues, anchor, high energy

Does inflate mean
to fill or to empty?

What do you call a female pig:
a sow or a boar?

Is a baby fox called
a kit or a chick?

Do bats sleep right-side up or upside down?

Which of these is a type of vegetable: a cucumber or a cuckooflower?

Is a tiny cabbage known as a Brussels sprout or potato sprout?

upside down, cucumber, Brussels sprout

Is a group of zebras called a hive or a herd?

What does the word "uno" mean in Spanish: one or many?

Is a lyre a garden tool or an instrument?

herd, one, instrument

Is the longest river in the United States the Missouri or the Mississippi?

What do you call an airplane that can land on the water: a seaplane or a sailplane?

Does a porcupine have spikes or quills?

Missouri, seaplane, quills

What did the tie say to the hat?

You go
on ahead
and I'll
hang around.

Is gold made from chemicals or dug from the ground?

What grows faster: your hair or your fingernails?

What should you drink to prevent heatstroke: soda or water?

dug from the ground, hair, water

Do supermodels walk on a catwalk or a dogwalk?

Are jellybeans grown in a garden or made in a factory?

If a job is called a "piece of cake" is it going to be easy or difficult?

Does fire require oxygen or helium to burn?

Do horses have the largest eyes or the largest teeth of any land animal?

Are robots complex or simple machines?

oxygen, eyes, complex

What can happen if you don't sleep enough: you grow taller or you get sick?

Do spiders lay eggs or give birth?

Which is the fastest animal in the world: the cheetah or the jaguar?

64

get sick, lay eggs, cheetah

Do snowshoes look more like tennis rackets or hockey sticks?

Which part of the Earth supports the continents: the crust or the mantle?

Does maple syrup come from a tree or an animal?

tennis rackets, crust, tree

Before pens were invented, did people write with quills and ink or berries and sticks?

Is a bookworm someone who likes to read or someone who likes to wiggle?

Which animal can see behind themselves without turning their heads: a rabbit or a wolf?

quills and ink, read, rabbit

Does a hurricane have a "tooth" or an "eye"?

Who is the leader of the United States: the senator or the president?

Is a butterfly a crustacean or insect?

eye, president, insect

Does toothpaste contain flour or fluoride?

Do tomatoes grow on a bush or a tree?

Are boas made of fur or feathers?

fluoride, bush, feathers

Do ants live as a group in a colony or alone by themselves?

Does submerge mean to descend below water or rise up above water?

Do acorns grow on trees or bushes?

colony, descend, trees

Which flavor are cats not able to taste: sweet or salty?

Do firefighters use arrows or axes to get into burning houses?

Which animal has teeth that never stop growing: a horse or a beaver?

sweet, axes, beavers

70

Why can't your nose be twelve inches long?

Because then it would be a foot!

If you round 264 to the nearest ten, do you get 260 or 270?

264

Is the world's stinkiest cheese from Finland or from France?

Which of these is an animal: coral or a mushroom?

260, France, coral

73

Which can you hear:
fog or hail?

Which plant is found in a pond:
a cactus or a cattail?

Are baby camels born
with or without humps?

74

hail, cattail, without

Are stars made
out of gas or rock?

Do bears eat
blueberries or grapes?

Which gender of toad croaks:
the male or the female?

gas, blueberries, male

75

Which part of a plant soaks up water: the flowers or roots?

Do you wash your hands to keep them soft or to prevent getting sick?

Which is the fastest animal that runs on two legs: an ostrich or a flamingo?

roots, prevent getting sick, ostrich

What does "hola" mean in the Spanish language: please or hello?

Is there more water or more land on the Earth's surface?

Are dogs known as man's best find or man's best friend?

hello, water, friend

77

Which is greater: 1111 or 1001?

How many states are there in the United States: 40 or 50?

What is the very center of a target called: the bull's eye or the cat's eye?

1111, 50, bull's eye

Which is attracted to a magnet: a pencil or a nail?

Is the city of Tokyo in Japan or China?

What do you get when you crush and grind grain: flour or sugar?

nail, Japan, flour

Is yoga a type of exercise or a type of furniture?

Is a shark a predator animal or prey animal?

Do tiaras dizzle or dazzle?

exercise, predator, dazzle

What is the main ingredient in an omelet: eggs or potatoes?

Does an eagle have toenails or talons?

Does a river have a "nose" or a "mouth"?

eggs, talons, mouth

Which is earlier: 10am or 1pm?

How many strings does a guitar have: three or six?

Which can run faster: a human or a hippo?

10am, six, hippo

What did the mother broom say to the baby broom?

It's time
to go
to sweep!

Does water freeze at 32 or 65 degrees Fahrenheit?

Which insect can jump the highest: grasshoppers or ants?

Are totem poles carved out of soap or wood?

32, grasshoppers, wood

Are balloons made out of rubber or wrapping paper?

Can bears see really far or smell really well?

Is a whale a mammal or a fish?

rubber, smell really well, mammal

Is a baby goat
called a pup or a kid?

Do teeth have roots or retinas?

Which of these fruits have pits:
peaches or kiwis?

kid, roots, peaches

87

Do humans breathe helium or oxygen?

Is a banana split a type of dessert or a gymnastics move?

What do people eat at Halloween: caramel cranberries or caramel apples?

oxygen, dessert, caramel apples

Do fruits and vegetables contain lots of fat or lots of vitamins?

Do snails leave behind a trail of mud or a trail of mucus?

Does jumping on a trampoline cause your body to burn pixels or to burn calories?

vitamins, mucus, calories

Does the word "timber" refer to rubber or wood?

Do crabs have a skeleton on the inside or outside of their bodies?

Who is known to have discovered mixing colors to form a new color: Plato or Pluto?

wood, outside, Plato

90

Are octopuses really smart or really furry animals?

Does solar refer to the sun or the moon?

What do you call a play that has songs in it: a musical or a tragedy?

smart, sun, musical

Is basketball played on a court or on a field?

Does clay come from a tree or from the ground?

Do hummingbirds make a humming sound with their wings or beaks?

court, ground, wings

Do bellhops work at hotels or hospitals?

Do people pay for groceries at a recorder or at a register?

In the French language, does "Bonjour" mean "I'm sorry" or "hello"?

hotels, register, hello

Are pyramids found in France or Egypt?

Does gravity pull objects up toward the sky or down toward the ground?

Which mineral is known as being the hardest: emeralds or diamonds?

Egypt, down, diamonds

What do you call a pig that does karate?

Porkchop!

Is a baby horse called
a foal or a lamb?

"Umbrella" in the Latin language
refers to what word:
rain or shade?

Which city is the
Golden Gate Bridge in:
Chicago or San Francisco?

foal, shade, San Francisco

Which of these animals has feathers: a viper or a vulture?

Which animal falls asleep standing up: a horse or a hedgehog?

Which number is greater than 1000: 999 or 1001?

1000

vulture, horse, 1001

Which word has more p's:
pepper or purple?

P

What is faster:
a helicopter or a car?

Which tree is used
for Christmas trees:
an evergreen or a maple?

pepper, helicopter, evergreen

Which instrument family does the trumpet belong to: the brass or the woodwind?

How many stars are on the American flag: 30 or 50?

Which word rhymes with toe: how or row?

brass, 50, row

100

Which animal has the largest eyes in the world: a squid or a whale?

Does a bowling ball weigh closer to 15 pounds or 50 pounds?

Are clouds made of tiny water drops or tiny tear drops?

squid, 15, water

Do daydreams happen when you are awake or when you are asleep?

Does water flow downhill or uphill?

As a candle burns, does it grow or shrink?

awake, downhill, shrink

Is the center of the Earth really cold or really hot?

Do sloths live in jungles or in deserts?

Do whales have lungs or gills?

really hot, jungles, lungs

103

Is the moon one temperature or does it change between hot and cold?

Which are stronger: your arms or your legs?

How long would it take to fly to Mars in a rocket: seven days or seven months?

it changes, legs, seven months

104

Which fish is used the most to make sushi: tuna or barracuda?

Who can see better at night: people or cats?

Which of these phrases is correct: "righty tighty, lefty loosey", or "righty mighty, lefty goosey"?

tuna, cats, righty tighty, lefty loosey

How fast can race cars go: 120 mph or 220 mph?

Do rivers flow into oceans, or do oceans flow into rivers?

Is the esophagus in your throat or ear?

220 mph, rivers flow into oceans, throat

What did the fish name his son?

Gill!

Which of these words is another word for surprise: startle or soothe?

Is your tongue the weakest or strongest muscle in your body?

Are giraffe legs around 6 feet tall or 12 feet tall?

startle, strongest, 6

Is a car closer to
15 feet long or 50 feet long?

Which animals don't have
brains: starfish or crabs?

Is a baby elephant called
a calf or a foal?

15 feet, starfish, calf

Is a tambourine a percussion instrument or a string instrument?

Is honeydew a fruit or a flower?

Are diamonds formed deep under ground from high pressure or above ground from low pressure?

percussion, fruit, high pressure

What do you call the liquid inside of a coconut: milk or juice?

Do police officers give tickets for driving too fast or for singing too loud?

Do peaches have many seeds inside or one big pit?

milk, driving fast, one big pit

Are beavers rodents or canines?

Does PB&J stand for peanut butter and jelly, or pickles, bacon, and juice?

How much money would it take to buy a car: 100 dollars or 10,000 dollars?

rodents, peanut butter and jelly, 10,000 dollars

Is the biggest state in America Rhode Island or Alaska?

Which animal is nocturnal: a raccoon or a squirrel?

Is a fold-up up bed called a kit or a cot?

Alaska, raccoon, cot

Which is the largest shark in the world: the whale shark or the great white shark?

Which of these has seeds: watermelons or carrots?

Are ballerinas graceful or clumsy?

whale shark, watermelons, graceful

115

Which animal can't move its eyeballs: an owl or a bat?

Which material would a t-shirt be made from: cornstarch or cotton?

What kind of scientist studies dinosaurs: a physiologist or a paleontologist?

owl, cotton, paleontologist

116

Is the smartest animal a monkey or a dog?

Do skunks protect themselves from predators by hiding in a shell or spraying a stinky scent?

Which of these words is a verb: swim or swimsuit?

monkey, spraying, swim

117

Is Mexico a country in
North America or South America?

Is a person who
studies planets and space
an astronomer or an astronaut?

To watch a bird in a tall tree,
should you use binoculars
or a magnifying glass?

North America, astronomer, binoculars

What did the pirate say on his 80th birthday?

Aye Matey!

80

Is a Mohawk a type of hairstyle or a type of bird?

Which dinosaur had three horns: ankylosaurus or triceratops?

Is a group of wolves called a pride or a pack?

hairstyle, triceratops, pack

Is pottery made
from plastic or clay?

What kind of animals
would you see at a zoo's
raptor show: birds or seals?

Is the
Statue of Liberty
made of
gold or copper?

clay, birds, copper

If you cut an apple into quarters, how many pieces would you have: two or four?

Are mangoes an exotic fruit or a hypnotic fruit?

Does beachcomb mean to look for shells, or put sand in your hair?

four, exotic, look for shells

123

Does a grasshopper or a butterfly hatch from a chrysalis?

Which are bigger: trolls or giants?

Which is a unit of weight: a kilometer or kilogram?

butterfly, giants, kilogram

Which of these is a type of cloud: nimbus or newton?

Do leprechauns hide gold at the end of rainbows or the end of rivers?

Are omnivores animals that eat plants, meat, or both plants and meat?

nimbus, rainbows, plants and meat

125

Which is colder:
the North Pole or South Pole?

Do lions live in Asia or Africa?

Is the width of the United States (coast to coast) roughly 270 miles or roughly 2,700 miles?

South Pole, Africa, 2,700 miles

126

Is a cartwheel a gymnastics move or a carnival ride?

Which word has the letter D at the end: sad or sat?

D

Do your lungs help you digest food or help you breathe?

gymnastics move, sad, breathe

Is light and fluffy snow
known as slush or powder?

What is a ray of light
from the moon called:
a moonstream or a moonbeam?

Do trees produce
oxygen or carbon dioxide?

powder, moonbeam, oxygen

Do birds fly in an arrow shape or circle shape?

Do all spiders have eight legs or six legs?

How many hours are in a day: 15 or 24?

arrow, eight, 24

Which time is the same as a quarter past two: 2:15 or 2:30?

Does a deer have horns or antlers?

Is a bat a bird or a mammal?

2:15, antlers, mammal

What did the beaver say to the tree?

It's been nice gnawing you!

How many legs would a team of four horses have: 15 or 16?

Do tractors paddle the ground or plow the ground?

Do sharks have bones or cartilage in their bodies?

16, plow, cartilage

133

Do peanuts grow above ground or under ground?

Do kangaroos live in Australia or Africa?

Can trees live for hundreds of years or thousands of years?

underground, Australia, thousands

Which direction is the opposite of east: north or west?

When someone says it's raining cats and dogs, do they mean it is raining hard, or they see animals in the sky?

Do male elk shed their antlers every year or every month?

west, raining hard, every year

Which dinosaur was known to fly: stegosaurus or pterodactyl?

Which ocean is smaller: the Atlantic or the Pacific?

Who painted the Mona Lisa: Leonardo da Vinci or Ludwig von Beethoven?

pterodactyl, Atlantic, da Vinci

Which melts ice faster: sugar or salt?

Is a beet a fruit or vegetable?

Does the earth have four seasons or six?

salt, vegetable, four

Which state are oranges grown in: Minnesota or Florida?

Is Monday part of a weekend or a weekday?

Do cherries grow on trees or bushes?

Florida, weekday, trees

What is larger:
a violin or a cello?

Which planet has rings:
Saturn or Mars?

Are the holes on the surface of the moon called critters or craters?

cello, Saturn, craters

Which dinosaur had sharp plates on its back: apatosaurus or stegosaurus?

What part of corn do we eat: the seeds or the leaves?

Which animal is known to show emotions: grasshoppers or gorillas?

stegosaurus, seeds, gorillas

Is an eclipse when the moon blocks the sun or when Mercury block the sun?

Is a group of turtles called a bunch or a bale?

How many planets are in the solar system: eight or ten?

moon, bale, eight

What animal helps to pollinate flowers: a bear or a bee?

Do beaver dams create ponds or lakes?

Does dinosaur mean "terrible lizard" or "hungry lizard?"

bee, ponds, terrible lizard

Why are ghosts bad liars?

Because you can see right through them!

Do pilots work in advertising or aviation?

Which holiday is celebrated with a menorah: Easter or Hanukkah?

How many lungs do you have: two or four?

aviation, Hanukkah, two

If you have 6 pairs of socks, do you have 14 or 12 individual socks?

Where is the Amazon River: in Belgium or Brazil?

In what sport do you jump on a trampoline: gymnastics or karate?

12, Brazil, gymnastics

146

Do flowers start to bloom in November or May?

Does water boil at 212 or 85 degrees Fahrenheit?

Do rivers grow when snow falls or when snow melts?

May, 212, melts

147

Does cheese come from goats or groundhogs?

Which dinosaur was bigger: a tyrannosaurus or a velociraptor?

Which animal is a predator to penguins: seals or polar bears?

148

goats, tyrannosaurus, seals

Who watches a penguin chick when it is first born: the mother or the father?

Does the U.S. President live in the White House or Orange House?

Do hermit crabs keep their shells for life or find new ones as they grow?

father, White House, new ones

How long does it take for light to travel from the sun to Earth: eight minutes or eight days?

Is karate a type of modern art or martial art?

Is a traditional Hawaiian dance called a hula or a tuba?

eight minutes, martial art, hula

Does corn grow on a stalk or a trunk?

What time is it if it is three hours after ten o'clock: one or two o'clock?

Which state is larger: Texas or Alaska?

stalk, one, Alaska

Do blackberry bushes have thorns or smooth vines?

Which planet is red: Mars or Jupiter?

Was skiing invented in Canada or Norway?

thorns, Mars, Norway

Which animals get sunburned: pigs or cows?

Which animal burrows underground: a squirrel or a groundhog?

What is the opposite of wild: crazy or tame?

pigs, groundhog, tame

Are airplanes aerobic or aerodynamic?

What is the deepest part of the Earth called: the crust or the core?

How many teeth does an alligator have: 10 or 80?

aerodynamic, core, 80

154

What did one eye say to the other?

Don't look now, but there's something smelly between us!

Is the longest day in the summer or the winter?

Are plastic bottles made from tree sap or from oil deep underground?

Which of these was invented first: the light bulb or the microwave?

summer, oil, light bulb

157

Is lightning a discharge of electricity or a discharge of fire?

Do cupcakes contain more salt or sugar?

Does poison ivy grow in the forest or at the beach?

electricity, sugar, forest

Is a mushroom a type of plant or a type of fungus?

Which is the biggest country in the world: China or Russia?

Is the earth spinning: yes or no?

fungus, Russia, yes

Is Earth five billion or five thousand years old?

Are clogs worn in China or the Netherlands?

Have astronauts landed on Jupiter or on the moon?

five billion years, Netherlands, moon

What is another word for flower: blossom or leaf?

Are pirates known as robbers of the salt or robbers of the sea?

Do flying helicopters detect nearby aircraft using sonar or radar?

blossom, robbers of the sea, radar

Is bluegrass a type of food or a type of music?

Are cranberries tart or sweet?

Is a moose's favorite food grass or caterpillars?

music, tart, grass

Does an animal's heart slow down when it is hibernating or hunting?

What animal lives longer: a mouse or a sea turtle?

Do butterflies hatch from a chrysalis or a crystal?

hibernating, sea turtle, chrysalis

Does the word "sidekick" refer to a good friend or an enemy?

What is a scientist called that studies rocks and minerals: a geologist or a meteorologist?

Which country has a maple leaf on its flag: Canada or Mexico?

good friend, geologist, Canada

Is the letter A a vowel or a consonant?

Do dogs cool down by panting or sweating?

Does a policeman enforce the laws or make the laws?

vowel, panting, enforce the laws

165

How many points do most starfish have: five or eight?

Is a ballroom a room for dancing or a room for bouncing balls?

Are grandmothers your mother's sister or your mother's mom?

five, dancing, mother's mom

166

If you were in a race and passed the person in second place, what place would you be in?

Second place!

Do the blue parts on a globe refer to water or land?

What month is Christmas in: December or September?

Which travels faster: light or sound?

water, December, light

What builds up on your teeth and gives you cavities: plaque or scales?

Which animal builds dams and lodges: a beaver or an otter?

How many holes do bowling balls have: three or five?

plaque, beaver, three

Which grows faster:
a bamboo tree or an oak tree?

Which of these is a plant:
a yucca or a ukulele?

When a bird flies south in the winter, is it called hibernation or migration?

bamboo, yucca, migration

When you reach a goal, do you feel triumphant or trumpeted?

Does the moon reflect light or absorb light?

Does the sun rise in the east or the south?

triumphant, reflect, east

Is the water in a pond moving or still?

How many eggs are in a half dozen: six or eight?

Which is a kind of dog: a Siamese or a retriever?

still, six, retriever

173

Does an herbivore
eat plants or meat?

Is the biggest animal on
the planet a blue whale
or an elephant?

Is a group of lions called
a gang or a pride?

plants, blue whale, pride

174

Do people sneeze with their eyes open or closed?

Does Bigfoot live in a forest or in a jungle?

Are dogs reptiles or mammals?

closed, forest, mammals

Which language uses "konnichiwa" to say hello: Japanese or Russian?

What would be an example of precipitation: rain falling from the sky or boiling water?

Is Australia known as the country "Down Under" or the country "Down Over"?

Japanese, falling rain, Down Under

Are canes used to walk with or to ski with?

Does divide mean to break apart or put together?

Does persistence mean: to keep trying or to give up easily?

walk, break apart, keep trying

Do mechanics fix cars or work in hospitals?

When fruit sits out for too long, does it spoil or splatter?

Is a shark a fish or a mammal?

What has a head and a tail but no body?

A coin!

Does irrigate mean to water plants or to pick fruit?

How much sleep should kids get each night: six hours or ten hours?

How much exercise should you get every day: 10 minutes or 60 minutes?

water plants, ten hours, 60

Which insect lives in large colonies: ants or crickets?

Are bulls male cows or male goats?

Do you cross your fingers for good luck or when you make a wish?

182

ants, male cows, good luck

How many people live
in the United States:
120 million or 320 million?

How many days of the week
start with the letter "T":
two or three?

Is "perimeter" the distance
around the outside of a shape
or a type of fruit?

320, two, distance

Does light enter a camera through the lens or the flash?

When you have no shoes on, do you have spare feet or bare feet?

What do you usually see before a rainstorm: dark clouds or sunshine?

lens, bare feet, clouds

What is 237 rounded to the nearest ten: 230 or 240?

237

Is your body made more of water or more of bone?

Which of these is an ocean: the Pacific or the Panama?

240, water, Pacific

185

Which is larger, 1/4 or 1/6?

Are most flags square-shaped or rectangle-shaped?

Which birds get nectar from a flower: hummingbirds or robins?

1/4, rectangular, hummingbirds

Which fish can't blink its eyes: a shark or a tuna?

Does a lily pad grow in an ocean or a pond?

When is it more likely to snow: January or July?

shark, pond, January

Which is longer:
an inch or a foot?

Before anchors were invented,
what was used to keep ships
in place: logs or rocks?

What part of a carrot do we
eat: the root or the leaves?

a foot, rocks, root

Is the planet Neptune
very hot or very cold?

How many continents are
there on Earth: 7 or 10?

How long does it take
for the Earth to travel
all the way around the Sun:
one month or one year?

very cold, 7, one year

Which of these is larger: a teaspoon or a tablespoon?

Does rotate mean to turn around or to cut in half?

Were triceratops herbivores or omnivores?

tablespoon, turn around, herbivores

190

What has four legs but can't walk?

A chair!

Is the highest temperature in a home kitchen oven around 500 degrees F or 1000 degrees F?

Does ascend mean to go up or to go down?

Do raisins come from grapes or oranges?

500, go up, grapes

What are you more likely to find in a hamburger: a cucumber or a pickle?

Which city is known as The Big Apple: Sydney or New York?

Do engines give airplanes thrush or thrust?

pickle, New York, thrust

Do wombats live
in Asia or Australia?

Which of these is
a pose in yoga:
shrub pose or tree pose?

Which is the most populated
city in the United States:
Los Angeles or New York?

Australia, tree pose, New York

Are baby sheep called foals or lambs?

How many square faces does a cube have: four or six?

Is a wishbone part of the elbow or collarbone in a turkey?

lambs, six, collarbone

Which of these is a secondary color: purple or yellow?

Do nurses work with pirates or patients?

Do doctors go to medical school or mechanic school?

purple, patients, medical school

197

What is harder:
a diamond or brick?

Does a carnivore eat
meat or plants?

Does a cat have
claws or talons?

diamond, meat, claws

Is a female fox called a vixen or a viper?

What is the closest planet to the sun: Mercury or Earth?

What color is raven: a shade of black or a shade of blue?

vixen, Mercury, black

Do snakes slither or slumber?

Which animal are you more likely to find living in a log: a squirrel or a mole?

Where are your taste buds: on your tongue or teeth?

slither, squirrel, tongue